Published in Australia 2005
Reprinted 2006
Publisher: Prudence Mapstone
Brisbane, Australia
Copyright © Prudence Mapstone

All rights reserved. No part of this publication may be reproduced, transmitted or stored in any form or by any means, electronic or mechanical, without prior written permission from the copyright holder.

www.knotjustknitting.com
prudence@knotjustknitting.com

ISBN 10: 0-9580443-2-5
ISBN 13: 978-0-9580443-2-5

Design & Photography by Dimity Mapstone

Printed by Kingswood Press
Brisbane, Australia

creating your own handbags

materials & techniques
for bag foundations

One of the major drawbacks with knitted or crocheted bags is that, unless they have had some form of very firm stiffening or stabilization added, they tend to droop and go out of shape as soon as they are made to carry any weight.

When designing your own one-of-a-kind handbag, one way to easily get around this problem would be to simply add some freeform embellishments to a pre-made bag.

Be on the lookout, especially at sales, for interesting or unusual shaped bags. Areas of knitting and crochet could be hot-glued on; or better still, if the bag is made from or covered with fabric, then your freeform pieces can be arranged over the surface and neatly stitched into place.

When constructing bags from scratch, you will probably need to add an extra layer of something firm between the outer fabric and the lining. For a small clutch bag, including an additional layer of stiff fabric or fleecy material may be all that is necessary to sufficiently firm up your purse.

Larger bags that are likely to carry more weight may require a firmer inter-lining. This could perhaps be made from canvas, stiff card, foam rubber, wood or plastic. Rug canvas or the sheets of plastic canvas normally used for embroidery and sold at craft stores are also suitable to use as an inter-lining.

materials & techniques

Pieces of mesh can be cut to shape, and then stitched together to produce handbags in all manner of interesting shapes and sizes. Individual crocheted or knitted motifs or freeform patches can be sewn onto the grid. If the spaces in the mesh are large enough, you can even crochet directly into or through the holes. Using fluffy or heavily textured yarns when working into or onto a mesh background will help you achieve good coverage.

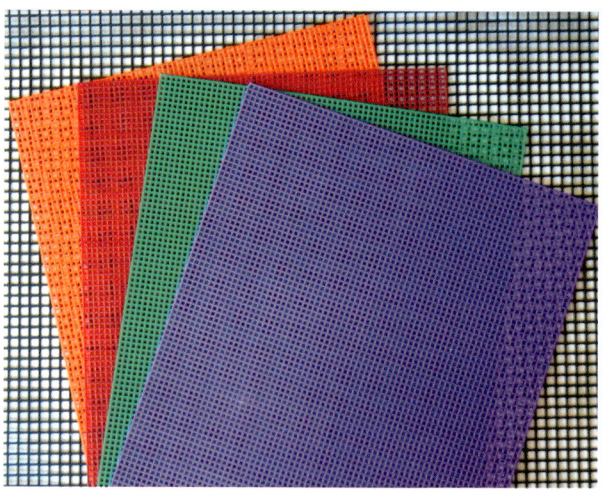

Any suitable material could become the foundation for a handbag. In this instance, a clear plastic sink drainer mat is being used as the base for a small clutch purse.

This bag is being made on a flat sheet of rug canvas. After the canvas was cut to size, one row of holes was folded inwards right around the piece. Then a row of dc (US: sc) stitches was made along two opposite edges. These borders have been crocheted using a feathery yarn so that the stitches cover the edges well. The crocheting was done from the wrong side (i.e. from the side that will become the inside of the bag) so that the texture of the yarn 'pops' towards the right side of the purse. The stitches have been worked into holes that are a couple of rows down from the edge and have been drawn up loosely, so as not to distort the canvas.

In the photo, a crochet chain is then being worked through the canvas to create a random pattern over the mesh. Note how the yarn is being picked up from behind the work and is being drawn through the holes from the back to the front. As you draw up each new loop, it must come not only through the mesh but also through the loop that is on your hook. Using an assortment of different yarns, the whole surface of this bag will eventually be covered in this manner.

materials & techniques

The best foundation I have used for handbags is a soft plastic mesh that is manufactured in Japan. It is available in flat sheets in various shapes and sizes, but also comes already 'bag-shaped'. This product is firm enough to hold its shape really well, without being so stiff that it is difficult to work onto.

This type of pre-shaped framework sells as a set comprising of two separate pieces. The front and back will at some stage need to be stitched together, and this can be done either before or after most of the covering and embellishment has been added. To date I have only ever found such a product in one size (see suppliers, p51), but the pieces can be cut, overlapped and stitched back together, to slightly alter the size and shape of the finished bag.

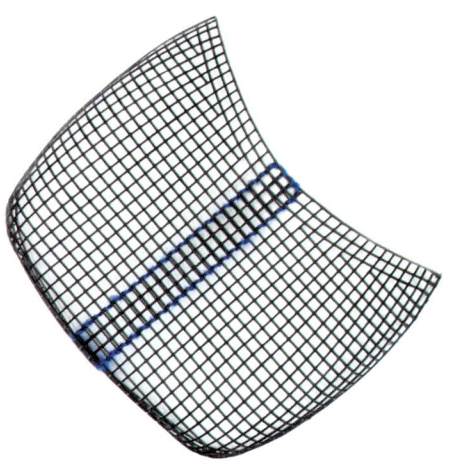

Cutting down the centre (lengthways) and overlapping a couple of rows of mesh will give a narrower bag, whilst cutting across the centre (widthways) will give a finished bag that is not quite so deep. To create yet another look you could also remove the curved rows of mesh at the top of the frame altogether.

Overlapping a row or two of holes before reassembling the pieces will give a much firmer and stronger bag than you would get if you were just to butt two sections together before rejoining. When assembling the front to the back, even if you haven't changed the size of the pieces, it is still always best to overlap one row of the mesh. Stitch along each side of the overlap for added strength.

These frames are flexible and easy to work with. They readily lend themselves to having random sections of freeform knitting and/or crochet attached. Since the holes in the mesh are large enough to take a medium weight yarn and hook, it is also possible to crochet directly into the plastic. You might like to do this to fill in small gaps between the patches. Crocheting into the mesh is also an easy way to create top borders, or to cover the base of the bag. Sometimes I stitch the two pieces of mesh together first, but at other times I find the mesh easier to work into when the two halves of the bag are still separate.

materials & techniques

Regardless of which type of framework or foundation you choose for your bag, whenever you are creating a fabric from a wide range of motifs, sections or patches, you will always want to arrange all of the separate elements in a pleasing manner.

Once you have made a number of pieces, begin to place them over your bag, but don't be in too much of a hurry to start joining them together immediately. Instead, move them around as you add each new piece, not only until they fit together well, but also until you are happy with the overall balance of colours, shapes and textures.

You can now either pin the pieces to each other, pin them all individually to the frame, or use a combination of both. Use long, straight pins or large safety pins. It is possible to attach the flatter and plainer sections with crochet. To do this, work through both the edge of the finished patch whilst at the same time also working into the holes in the foundation mesh. When crocheting patches on in this way it is best to use a somewhat fluffy yarn. The more 'untidy' the yarn the better the coverage, as the texture will help to disguise any messy joins or slightly uneven stitches.

If you have created any three-dimensional sections, they will generally need to be carefully hand-sewn into place. Work with the right side facing. Make most of your stitches into the side edge of each piece as you connect them to each other, but sometimes also take the needle down through the mesh so that you are attaching things to the frame as well. By sewing everything together from the right side, you can easily check that none of your stitches are going to show on the surface. It will also help ensure that you stitch under and behind any areas that should remain raised.

designideas for freeform projects

Simple Random Stripes

One of the easiest methods for jazzing up a store-bought bag is to add some simple stripes, worked in either knitting or crochet, using a variety of exciting yarns. First, choose your pre-made bag. It will be easier to calculate the amount of knit or crochet fabric you require if the bag is a fairly simple design - one where you will be covering just a square or rectangular area.

Select a number of different yarns. You might like to include some that have been left over from other projects, but make sure that all of the colours go together well, and that they also tone in with any parts of the bag that will be left exposed. Use both smooth and fancy yarns, so that each acts as a foil for the other. The inclusion of one or two fringed or eyelash yarns will help to blend the colour changes subtly.

All of your yarns do not have to be of exactly the same weight. For this design you will be working a series of single row stripes. When you alternate yarns that are of slightly different thicknesses, the overall tension will generally even itself out, although in some instances you may wish to combine two much thinner threads together. This often works particularly well if you use a fine baby-weight or sock-weight yarn along with the type of eyelash that is spun onto a thin thread binder.

Using knitting needles or a crochet hook in a size that approximately suits the average weight of the yarns you have chosen, knit or crochet a small tension square or swatch. Use each yarn for just one row at a time before changing to another. Make your swatch in the same stitch pattern that you intend to use for the bag. The example in the photo was simply done in knitted garter stitch (i.e. every row was worked in Knit stitches). Since garter stitch doesn't curl in at the edges, it is easy to measure and calculate the number of stitches required. When you work <u>each row in a different colour</u>, the resulting fabric will appear to have no obvious right or wrong side. This was an advantage when the same combination of yarns and stitch pattern was used to make the matching scarf, as it is fully reversible.

Once you have made your swatch, lay it out flat, measure it, and calculate the approximate number of stitches and rows that it will take to cover the chosen area.

If you are intending to attach your created fabric to a fairly firm bag, it is usually best to make the finished piece just slightly smaller than the area to be covered. If the knitted or crocheted fabric is stretched a little to ease it into place as it is stitched to the bag, it will be much less likely to droop or go out of shape with wear.

Once you have estimated how many stitches and rows you will need, knit or crochet your striped fabric. Try to alternate the smooth and fancy (or the thicker and thinner) yarns, to achieve a good overall balance.

If you decide to make your fabric using a stitch pattern that has a definite right and wrong side, it is nearly always preferable to work any textured yarns for 'wrong side facing' rows only. This is because irregularities in the yarn, such as slubs, bumps, fringes and eyelashes, will usually want to stay to the back of the work as you knit or crochet. Therefore it follows that when you work them from the wrong side you will keep most of the textural interest on the right side.

If you normally work tightly, you may find that the long, loose strands in some novelty yarns get caught up in your work. Once you have finished the piece, use the point of a knitting needle or blunt bodkin to gently flip the eyelashes to the surface on the right side.

designideas

Freeform additions to Fabric

For this silk bag with flap closure, a single piece of soft plastic mesh was cut to the width and double the desired height of the bag. Next, a piece of woven silk fabric was cut larger than the piece of mesh. The fabric for this style of bag will need to be at least 20cm (8") wider and approximately half as long again as the height of the piece of mesh (to allow enough fabric for the flap and the gussets).

Lay the fabric down and place the mesh on top, turning over approximately 5 cm (2") of fabric at one end. Pin the fabric into place at that end. Fold the mesh gently in half (the bottom of the bag will now softly curve), and pin the fabric into place across the other end of the mesh. Fold the remaining fabric over to produce a flap. Leaving sufficient fabric to allow for a small hem on the edge of the flap, cut the end of the fabric into a curved shape if desired. Turn in the edge along the curved part of the flap, pin into place and tack the hem.

Using a toning yarn (in this case, some hand-spun recycled silk from Nepal), create a straight piece of soft, reasonably loose knitting or crochet that is long enough and wide enough to cover the edge of the flap. Provided that the curved edge is not too deep and you work at a tension that produces a fairly pliable fabric, you should be able to ease this straight piece of knitting or crochet smoothly around the edge of the flap. Fan it out or bunch it up slightly, as may be needed to smoothly follow the line of the curve. Pin into position on the front of the flap, then fold the edging in half lengthways, back under the flap, and stitch it neatly into place.

Turn the side edges inwards, and pin the top of the front and back together on each side. I often find that if I gently ease the fabric outwards as I pin it downwards towards the bottom of the bag, I can pleat it and neatly form a gusset using just the spare fabric at the edges. This saves having to create a specially shaped piece to fit at the sides. Once I have the fabric pinned to my liking, it can be neatly hand-stitched into position. This type of bag can then also be embellished further with areas of freeform knitting and/or crochet, or with interesting buttons and beads.

For the bag on the left below, a purchased pre-strung beaded fringe has been dropped through the holes in the mesh and will be stitched into place before the covering is added. For the bag on the right, areas of knitted and crocheted fabric were arranged to completely cover a piece of flat mesh. In both cases, the mesh was folded in half, allowing the bottom of the bags to softly curve. Small teardrop-shaped areas can be created, using either knitting or crochet, in the size and shape required to fit into the gaps at the sides of bags such as these, and then used as gussets.

designideas
Covering with Freeform Patches

You can also fully cover pre-made fabric bags or mesh frames using a varied array of knit and/or crochet stitches made with a range of different yarns. You will not need to initially worry about the measurement of the finished piece if you first create many individual motifs or very small patches.

As you make the pieces or patches, place them on top of the bag and move them around. Fit them together like a jigsaw puzzle, and when you are happy with the overall placement, pin them into position. The manner in which you assemble everything is now up to you.

One possibility would be to stitch the patches directly to the base, at the same time catching them to each other as you work. Or perhaps you would prefer to pin all of the pieces just to each other, forming a continuous section of fabric the size and shape of the area you wish to cover. Once this is done, you can then lift the pinned fabric from the bag, sew everything together, and then fit the completed fabric back over the foundation again, finally stitching it into place around the edges. As mentioned previously, to ensure a neat, firm fit it is often best if the fabric is made just slightly smaller than the size of the area it needs to cover.

If you feel that the freeform fabric needs to be caught down further to keep it secure, consider using fancy embroidery stitches or attaching the occasional button or bead where needed, so that these elements also become part of the overall design.

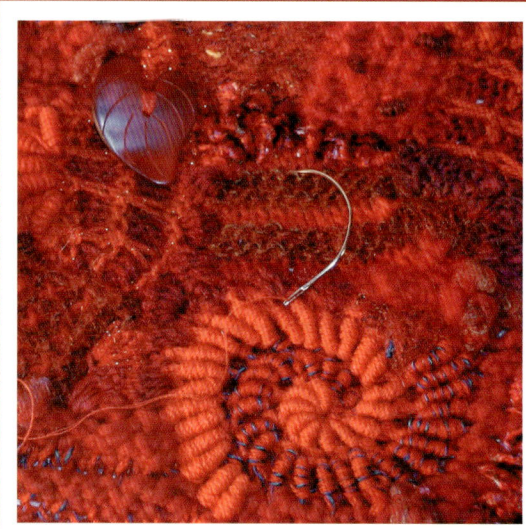

Using a curved upholstery needle will often make the final stitching less difficult, especially if you are attaching your work to a pre-made bag where the base fabric is closely woven or very firmly attached.

Creating Freeform Fabrics

If you have never tried your hand at making freeform knitted or crocheted fabrics before, begin by working just very small areas at a time – less than about 5cm (2"). Cast on your stitches or make a chain, work a few rows, and finish off. Do not just continue on in the same direction. Instead pick up stitches from the side edge or the corner of the previous piece and add on another small area, using a different yarn and a different stitch pattern. Again work a few rows and finish off. If you are proficient at both knitting and crochet, combine both crafts within each patch.

Sometimes for small projects you may feel that you will be able to manipulate the stitches so that they do exactly as you wish while you are working. If that is the case, you might choose to continue to add to the piece until it is the desired size. If you are doing this, you will need to periodically place the work over the area that you will be covering, so that you can be sure you are creating your fabric to the correct shape.

At other times you may find it much easier to create many individual pieces or small sections in a variety of random shapes. Once you have sufficient motifs and patches, all of these pieces can then be fitted together, again using the bag as a template.

I usually prefer to make many smallish pieces, which I then arrange and rearrange over the bag frame until I am completely happy with the way the design has come together. Next, the individual sections are pinned onto the bag, edge to edge, using large safety pins. Using a smooth, toning yarn I then hand-stich the pieces to each other and into place. I prefer to use mattress (ladder) stitch, and to work from the right side. I sew from the edge of one piece to the edge of another for a few stitches and occasionally take the needle down through the frame or foundation, so that I catch the fabric into place there as well.

designideas

Organic Handbags

Organic freeform knit and crochet handbags such as these can be created from many individual flower and leaf motifs. Make these separately in different sizes and shapes using simple patterns and interesting yarns.

Once you have a good selection of motifs made, begin to arrange them onto your bag template, temporarily pinning them into place. Add more motifs as you make them, but still be prepared to move everything around - not only until you have made enough motifs to cover the whole area, but also until you are satisfied with the overall design.

designideas

motif patterns
& adaptations
that you might like to try

The following 'patterns' provide suggestions for many different motif shapes to get you started. Do not feel that you are limited to using only these. Try to create your own variations, as well as incorporating any other shapes and designs you may find in books or on the internet, so that the bag you create will be truly unique.

Knitted Leaf Motif
with Surface Crochet

Cast on 2 or 3 stitches and knit 1 row. Increase into the first stitch on the next row. Knit the next row. Increase into the first stitch on the next row. Knit a few more rows. Increase at one end or the other of the following row (you decide which). Knit a few more rows without further shaping.

Continue working in garter stitch (i.e. knitting each row). Do not increase on every row (we are aiming for a leaf-like shape here, not a triangle), but randomly make an increase on one side or the other <u>only when you feel that it is needed</u> to form a pleasing shape, continuing in this manner until the piece is the desired <u>width</u>.

Now work a number of rows with no shaping (approximately 6 to 12 or even more rows, depending on the size of the leaf you wish to create). Keeping an eye on how your leaf is progressing, randomly decrease the stitches back down towards a point again by knitting together at either the beginning or end of some, but not all, of the rows (again, this is your choice). The rate at which you work the decreases does not necessarily need to be the same as the rate of the increase rows.

When your leaf is complete, choose a toning yarn of approximately the same weight, and work some further embellishment.

With the right side of the piece facing towards you, the yarn at the back of the work and the hook at the front, pull through a loop of yarn at one end of the leaf. Continue pulling loops up through the knitted fabric plus at the same time through the centre of the previous loop, forming a row of chain stitches that follows a random, winding path down the centre of the leaf to resemble a vein, as was done for the leaf on page 22. If desired, additional small veins can also be worked outwards from this central line of crochet. Note that you probably will not be able to tell the front from the back on your garter stitch knitting, but if you ever wish to add this type of surface crochet onto a piece that has a definite right and wrong side, then the yarn will need to be held behind the work (i.e. on the wrong side), and the hook will be held at the front (right side).

Other methods for decorating the tops of leaves could include:

Crocheting onto the surface (from the right side), working a ridge of dc (US: sc) stitches, or

Using crochet crab stitch (US: reverse sc) on the surface to form an even more pronounced vein, as was done for the leaves on the right.

When working onto the surface of your motifs in this manner, you will find it easiest if you first fold the leaf down the centre, and work your crochet stitches into this 'false' edge. To look organic, the stitches will not want to just follow a straight line, so change the direction of the fold periodically.

motif patterns

Small Crochet Leaf Motif

Make 12 chain.

Row 1: 1 dc (US: 1 sc) into the 2nd ch from hook, 1 dc (US: 1 sc) into the next ch, 1 htr (US: 1 hdc) into each of the next two ch, 1 tr (US: 1 dc) into each of the next 3 ch, 2 tr (US: 2 dc) into the next ch, 2 htr (US: 2 hdc) into the next ch, 1 htr (US: 1 hdc) into the next ch, 1 sl st into the last ch.

Do not turn the work, but carefully make the following row behind each of the stitches of the foundation chain, so that as you work you are also forming a central ridge down the middle of the leaf, between the two rows of stitches:

Row 2: 1 dc (US: 1 sc) behind the first st, 1 dc (US: 1 sc) behind the next st, 1 htr (US: 1 hdc) behind each of the next two sts, 1 tr (US: 1 dc) behind each of the next 3 sts, 2 tr (US: 2 dc) behind the next st, 2 htr (US: 2 hdc) behind the next st, 1 htr (US: 1 hdc) behind the next st, 1 sl st into the last st. Fasten off.

Make a few more leaves in this manner. Once you feel confident that you understand the principles involved in creating a crochet motif with this type of shape, try working other similar leaves along different length chains, perhaps incorporating some taller stitches or a second round. When working additional rounds or stitches, make sure that you work a couple of extra stitches at each of the points, to ensure there is enough ease to go around the curves without puckering the work.

motifpatterns
Corkscrew Flower Motif made with either knitting or crochet

Two separate 2-row corkscrew motifs, twisted into a number of different configurations to produce various floral motifs.

Corkscrews in Crochet

Make a length of chain (approximately 20 ch long). Work 3 dc (US: 3 sc) into each ch to the end and finish off, leaving a length of yarn long enough for sewing.

Starting at one end, carefully roll the motif up so that it resembles a flower, keeping the centre section tight and loosening up towards the outermost round. Stitch the motif together at the base, being sure to catch each round securely.

Thicker corkscrews (and therefore taller flowers) can be made by substituting htr (US: hdc), tr (US: dc) or dtr (US: tr) stitches for the dc (US: sc) stitches in this pattern. Alternatively begin with short stitches at one end of the row and gradually move on to taller stitches – for example, work approximately the first third of the length of the chain in dc (US: sc), the next third in htr (US: hdc) and the last third in tr (US: dc) stitches.

Sometimes you may wish to work an additional row of stitches, perhaps using a contrasting colour. The second row of stitches can be of a different height to the first. If your initial row only produced a loose corkscrew, you could work two stitches into each of the stitches in the first row to force it to twist more tightly. You might also sometimes like to add a row of crochet picots along the length of the basic corkscrew by working a second row as follows:

1 dc (US: 1 sc) into the first st, then *1 dc, 3 ch, 1 dc (US: 1 sc, 3 ch, 1 sc) into the next st., 1 dc (US: 1 sc) into the next st.   Repeat from * to the end of the row.

Corkscrews in Knitting

Cast on approximately 20 stitches. Knit 1 row. Increase into every stitch in the next row (i.e. knit into the front and back of each stitch before slipping the stitch off the needle - thereby doubling the number of stitches in the row). Repeat this row at least once more. Cast off (US: bind off). Roll the finished piece to form a flower shape and stitch, as per the crochet instructions.

You can also vary the size of knitted corkscrew flowers in many ways, such as by beginning with a different number of stitches, by increasing more times into each stitch, or by working more increase rows. For tiny, less three-dimensional flowers, work one increase row only, but knit into each stitch along that row 4 or 5 times.

motif patterns

Crochet Ruffled Flower Motif

Choose 3 different yarns – this motif is often most effective when a smooth yarn is used for the 1st (centre) round, and a thinner or lighter weight yarn is used for the 3rd (outside) round.

<u>1st round</u>: Make 3 ch and join with a sl st to form a small ring, then make 3 more ch. Now work approximately 12 tr (US: 12 dc) into the ring. Join with a sl st into the top of the 3 ch to close, and finish off the 1st yarn.

<u>2nd round</u>: Join in the 2nd colour, make 3 ch, and then work approximately 3 tr (US: 3 dc) into each of the tr (US: dc) of the previous round. Close with a sl st and finish off the 2nd yarn.

<u>3rd round</u>: Join in a 3rd yarn, make 1 ch, and then work 2, 3 or more dc (US: 2, 3 or more sc) into each of the tr (US: dc) of the previous round. Close with a sl st.

The more stitches you work in each round, the more ruffled your flowers will be. If you want your flowers to become more ruffled, but think that the yarn you are using will make them too stiff, add a chain or two between each of the stitches.

To vary some of these flowers slightly, you could turn the piece over and work the 3rd round with the wrong side of the motif facing towards you. This is especially effective when you choose to work the last round using a thin but fuzzy or textured yarn.

Sometimes you might like to substitute a row of picots for the 3rd round, working them in the same manner as given for the Crochet Corkscrew flowers.

Crochet Bullion Circle

Work 3 ch and join with a sl st to form a small ring, then work approximately 3 more ch.

*Evenly wind the yarn 5 or more times around the shaft of the hook. Insert the hook into the small ring, yarn over hook and draw the yarn through the loops until just two loops are left on the hook, then yarn over hook and draw through the remaining two loops.

Repeat from * approximately 11 times more. Join with a slip stitch into the top of the 3 ch to close.

For tips that will make the Bullion Stitch easy to work, plus lots of ideas for incorporating many other bullion motifs into your freeform design work, see my book 'Bullions & Beyond' - details on page 50.

motifpatterns

Crochet Spiral with Surface Detail

For the type of spiral motif used in this bag, firstly a single colour background is made for each individual motif. Each is then embellished with further rounds of crochet, which are worked onto the surface using either the same or a different yarn.

For a detailed explanation of the crochet block stitch braid that has been used for the handle on this bag, visit my website for a downloadable PDF instruction booklet.

Spiral Background

Using any smooth yarn, make 3 ch and join with a sl st to form a small ring. Make 3 additional ch, and then work approximately 12 tr (US: 12 dc) into the small ring. DO NOT close the round with a sl st, but now begin to work outwards in a spiralling manner as follows:

Work 2 tr (US: 2 dc) into the back loop of each of the 3 additional ch sts that you made after forming the ring, and then work 2 tr (US: 2 dc) into the <u>back loop only</u> of each of the tr (US: dc) of the preceding round. (**Note that** working into the back loops only will leave all of the front loops free to act as a guide for the surface stitches to be worked later. To avoid small holes forming and to help keep the stitches firm, you may wish to work your stitches into both the back loop and also at the same time into the loop below at the back of the work).

When you have done a complete circuit in this manner and so that the motif remains flat, you will need to reduce the frequency of the increases, by working the next round as follows:

Work 2 tr (US: 2 dc) into the back loop of the first tr (US: dc) of the preceding round, then work 1 tr (US: 1 dc) into the back loop of the next, then 2 tr (US: 2 dc) into the back loop of the next tr (US: dc), then 1 tr (US: 1 dc) into the back loop of the next. Continue in this manner, i.e. increasing only in every second stitch in this round. Finish off at the completion of this round, or if you wish you could work the last 6 to 8 or so stitches as htr (US: hdc) then dc (US: sc) then slip stitches, to ease the edge of the motif down into a smooth circle shape before finishing.

Surface Detail

With the <u>right side</u> of the motif facing you and the <u>yarn at the front of the work</u>, join your yarn back into the centre of the circle. If you decide to use a different yarn for the surface stitches, it is often best to choose one that is not any thicker than the background yarn or it will overpower the background. Following the ridge of front loops from the centre to the outside edge, work 1 dc (US: 1 sc) into each loop.

Should you ever wish to make a larger spiral, each subsequent round will need to have one extra stitch between each of the increases if you wish the motif to continue to lie flat (i.e. you should always only need to increase a total of approximately 12 stitches in each round). Therefore the third round would be as follows: work 2 tr (US: 2 dc) into the back loop of the first tr (US: dc) of the preceding round, then work 1 tr (US: 1 dc) into the back loop of each of the next <u>two</u> stitches. A fourth round would be: work 2 tr (US: 2 dc) into the back loop of the first tr (US: dc) of the preceding round, then work 1 tr (US: 1 dc) into the back loop of the next <u>three</u> stitches, and so forth.

motifpatterns

Spiral Flower Motif

After creating a spiral background section as before, it is simple to turn this type of design into a flower motif by working the surface detailing as follows:

Using either thread or a very thin yarn, follow the ridge of front loops from the centre to the outside edge, this time working 4 or more dc (US: sc) into each of the loops, to create a ruffled effect on the surface. For a taller ruffle, substitute tr (US: dc) stitches. Alternatively start with short stitches at the centre of the motif and gradually increase the height of the stitches as you work towards the outside, or work a greater number of stitches into each loop once you reach the outer edge of the motif.

Knitted Windmill Flower

Special abbreviation to prevent small holes forming in your work as you make the short rows: When the pattern says **"turn"**: take the yarn to the front of the work, slip the next stitch purlwise, take the yarn to the back of the work, turn the work, slip the stitch purlwise back onto the original needle, take the yarn to the back of the work.

Cast on 12 stitches
Row 1: Knit 7 stitches, "turn"
Row 2: Knit 3, "turn"
Row 3: Knit 4, "turn"
Row 4: Knit 5, "turn"
Row 5: Knit 6, "turn"
Row 6: Knit 7, "turn"
Row 7: Knit 8, "turn"
Row 8: Knit 7, "turn"
Row 9: Knit 6, "turn"
Row 10: Knit 5, "turn"
Row 11: Knit 4, "turn"
Row 12: Knit 8 stitches (that is, to the end of the row)
Row 13: Cast off (US: bind off) leaving the last stitch on the needle
*Cast on 11 stitches (you will now have 12 stitches on the needle)

Repeat Rows 1 to 13, plus the cast on row with the *, five more times (6 petals made)

Slip the last stitch off the needle and onto a crochet hook, and connect the petals to form the centre of the flower as follows:

Put the hook into the base of the first petal, yarn over hook and draw the loop through
* Put the hook into the base of the next petal, yarn over hook and draw the loop through
Repeat from * for each petal in turn (you will now have 7 loops on the hook)
Yarn over hook and draw through all of the loops
Cut yarn, draw through remaining loop to finish.

Thread the end of the yarn onto a sewing needle and catch the base of the petals to each other at the back of the work with a few stitches to firm up the completed motif, if needed.

motif patterns

Tri-colour Crochet Flower

Make 3 ch and join with a sl st to form a small ring. Work 3 more ch, then work 11 tr (US: 11 dc) into the centre of the ring. Slip stitch into the top of the 3 ch to close, and finish off the first colour.

Now turn the work to the wrong side, join in a 2nd colour, and proceed as follows:
*Into the next stitch work 1 dc (US: 1 sc)
Into the next stitch work [2 htr (US: 2 hdc) 1 tr (US: 1 dc) 2 htr (US: 2 hdc)]. Repeat from * 5 times. Join with a sl st to close and finish off the second colour.

Still with the wrong side facing, place your hook through the edge of the centre circle at a position between two petals, and draw through a loop of the 3rd yarn, and make 1 loose dc (US: 1 loose sc).
*Work 1 dc (US: 1 sc) into each of the next 2 htr (US: the next 2 hdc) of the previous round, work 2 dc (US: 2 sc) into the next tr (US: the next dc), work 1 dc (US: 1 sc) into the next 2 htr (US: the next 2 hdc). Work 1 loose dc (US: 1 loose sc) right down into into the edge of the centre circle between the petals. Repeat from * right around the motif, omitting the last loose dc (US: sc) and instead joining with a sl st to close.

The petals on this flower will turn downwards. If you do all the rows from the right side, the petals will cup (i.e. turn upwards).

motif patterns

Some suggestions for Underwater theme bags

For this bag, a knitted stocking stitch background was first created. Loosely woven knit fabric could be substituted. To achieve the look of seaweed, textured yarns were then crocheted through the knitting. This was done in the same manner as the veins on the leaves on page 23. Various motifs, including those following, were made and applied to the surface. The fabric was then stitched to the foundation, which in this case was created from two large rectangles and three narrow strips, cut from plastic canvas and then stitched together.

Little Crochet Fishies

Make 14 ch. Miss the 1st ch and proceed as follows: Work 1 sl st into each of the next 2 ch, 1 dc (US: 1 sc) into each of the next 6 ch, 1 htr (US: 1 hdc) into each of the next 2 ch, 1 dc (US: 1 sc) into each of the next 2 ch, then into the last ch work [1 dc, 1 ch, 1 dc (US: 1 sc, 1 ch, 1 sc)]

Do not turn the work but continue back down the other side of the ch as follows:

Work 1 dc (US: 1 sc) into the first 2 ch, 1 htr (US: 1 hdc) into the next 2 ch, then 1 dc (US: 1 sc) into each of the next 4 ch.

For the other side of the tail, make 4 ch, miss the 1st ch, work 1 sl st into the next ch, 1 dc (US: 1 sc) into each of the next 2 ch, 1 sl st into the next ch, and then sl st into the centre of the tail to close and finish off.

Embroider an eye if desired, or stitch on a small bead.

Knitted Tropical Fish

Make a slip knot, and knit into it twice.
Increase into the first stitch, knit the next stitch.
Increase into the first stitch, knit to the end of the row.
Repeat this last row 7 times (11 sts).
Cast on 3 stitches at the beginning of the next row, knit to the end of the row (14 sts).
Cast on 2 stitches at the beginning of the next row, knit to the end of the row (16 sts).
Repeat this last row once more (18 sts).
Increase into the first stitch, knit to the end of the row (19 sts).
Cast off (US: bind off) 5 stitches (fairly tightly), knit to the end of the row.
Cast off (US: bind off) 4 stitches (fairly tightly), knit to the end of the row.
Knit 8 rows, with no further shaping, on these 10 stitches.
Knit 2 stitches together right across this next row (5 sts)
Cast on 4 stitches at the beginning of the next row, knit to the end of the row (9 sts).
Repeat this last row once more (13 stitches).
Cast on 2 stitches at the beginning of the next row, knit to the end of the row (15 sts).
Repeat this last row once more (17 sts).
Cast off (US: bind off) - (again, fairly tightly, to help shape the tail).
Embroider an eye if desired, or stitch on a small bead.

Basic Two-colour Spiral

Choose two contrasting yarns of approximately the same weight. Using Colour 1, make 3 ch and join with a sl st to form a small ring. Make 3 more ch, and work approximately 6 tr (US: 6 dc) into the ring. Pull up a long loop by loosening the loop that is on the hook, and remove the hook. Join Colour 2 into the centre of the small ring, make 3 ch, and work approximately 6 tr (US: 6 dc) into the ring. Still using Colour 2 and again working the increases as in the previous spiral motifs (i.e. with a total of approximately 12 increases in each round), begin to spiral up the 3 ch and then into the tops of the stitches that were made with Colour 1. When you run out of stitches into which you can work, pull up a long loop and remove the hook and then go back to once again using the previous colour. Continue in this manner until your motif is the desired size, being sure to only make approximately 12 increases in each round if you wish the motif to stay flat.

Spiral Variations

Oval Spirals
Work all of the increases into stitches that are together on opposite sides of the motif, and work all of the single stitches together along what will soon become the long edges.

Spirals with more than 2 colours
To create spirals motifs with more than two colours, divide 12 by the number of colours you wish to use, and begin with an equal number of stitches in each colour in the first round (i.e. 4 initial sts in each colour if working in 3 colours; 3 sts in each for 4 colours).

Bullion Spirals

Following the same principle as for the basic two-colour spiral, begin a spiral in which all of the stitches made with colour 1 are bullion stitches (with approximately 5 wraps), and all of the stitches made with colour 2 are tr (US: dc).

Or follow the same principle as for the two-colour spiral above made with bullions and tr (US: dc) sts, but throughout the course of this spiral gradually increase the number of wraps made for the bullions as follows:

Begin with approximately 4 wraps for the first 3 to 5 bullion stitches, and then increase the number by one wrap every 3 to 5 stitches until the end. This motif will resemble a nautilus shell. You can also very gradually either increase or decrease the height of the other stitches as well. Additional crochet can also be added, either onto or through the stitches in this motif, for further embellishment.

Some hints
for **attaching the motifs** to mesh frameworks
and for **finishing your freeform bags**

When using the pre-formed frames, if you wish to reduce the height or width of the handbag-shaped mesh sections, cut each section either down or across the centre row of holes, overlap a row or two, and whip stitch the pieces together using a smooth yarn in a shade that tones with the overall colour scheme. For an evening bag I sometimes like to change the shape of the frame by cutting off the curved rows of plastic at the top of the mesh.

You will often find that assembling your bag is easiest if you firstly attach most of the motifs onto the individual sections of the mesh framework before the two sections are stitched together.

Place the motifs onto each half of the bag frame separately, and move them around until you are pleased with the overall arrangement of shapes, colours and textures.

Depending on the style of handle you choose to use, decide whether it would be best and/or easiest to attach the handles early or late in the construction process.

Pin each of the motifs into place using large safety pins. For stability it is best if you overlap one row of holes at the edges of the mesh when you stitch the pieces together, so do not initially stitch your motifs all the way to the side or bottom borders of either of the sections. You can have some areas of your work pinned ready to go beyond their own side of the mesh, provided that a corresponding space is left free to accommodate the piece on the other side.

You can choose to take your motifs right to the top edge of the mesh, or you may prefer to leave a row or two of holes free, so that you can crochet a continuous band of stitches right around the top edge either before or after the two sections of the bag have been stitched together. This is usually best done using a fringed or highly textured yarn, so that the stitches will fully cover the mesh.

You may need to create some extra small pieces to fill in any holes in your design. Random hand stitching using a textured yarn is also a good way to fill in any very small spaces where the mesh may show.

some hints

You could perhaps decide to crochet directly into the framework to cover the base of the bag, if you do not wish to place your more complex motifs where they really wouldn't be seen. Remember that the edge rows of mesh will need to overlap, so leave this area free until after the two sections of the bag are finally assembled. Or stitch the frame together first, and crochet around the oval design of the base, working your stitches in a series of continuous rounds.

Stitch the motifs and patches directly onto the mesh using a toning yarn, or crochet some parts of some of the patches into place by working through the patch and at the same time also into the mesh. Do not just totally outline any one piece using the same yarn, but add more visual interest by partly surrounding the patches with a number of different yarns.

When you have most of the pieces in place, pin the two sections of the bag together. Be sure to overlap one row of mesh. Work two rows of whipstitching to join the pieces securely.

Stitch down any patches that overlap from one side to the other. Make additional small motifs in either knitting or crochet to fit into any gaps that are left along the seams, or cover the joins with areas of random crochet worked into the mesh using a fringed or very textured yarn.

If you wish to line your handbag, fold a piece of fabric and generously cut it to a size that will loosely fit inside the frame. Pin the fabric into shape and stitch the side seams. Place the lining into the bag and fold the top edge over, back towards the mesh. Pin it into position, making small pleats around the top if needed to get a good fit. Hand-stitch the lining neatly to the inside of the mesh using a matching thread. Catch the fabric in place at the bottom of the bag if desired.

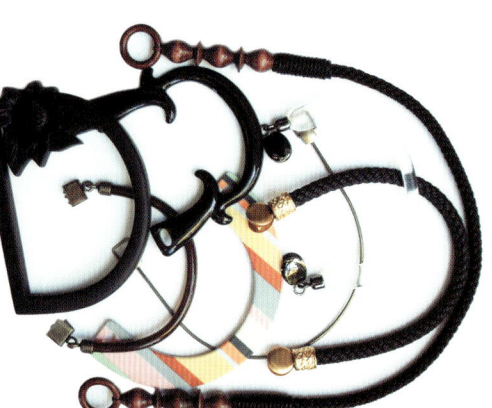

Because you will be using your own choice of foundation, stitch patterns, yarns and other embellishments for each bag that you make, working in a freeform manner will give you the flexibility to adapt any of the techniques in this book to suit your own particular needs, design ideas and materials. Experimenting and making any necessary adjustments along the way will therefore always result in a truly 'original' piece of wearable art.

Further Embellishment Ideas

Wire-edged ribbon makes an interesting addition

Use unusual buttons and buckles for closures

Embellishment with beads and unique wooden handles

A drawstring closure for a circular bag where the freeform work was attached to gutter guard mesh

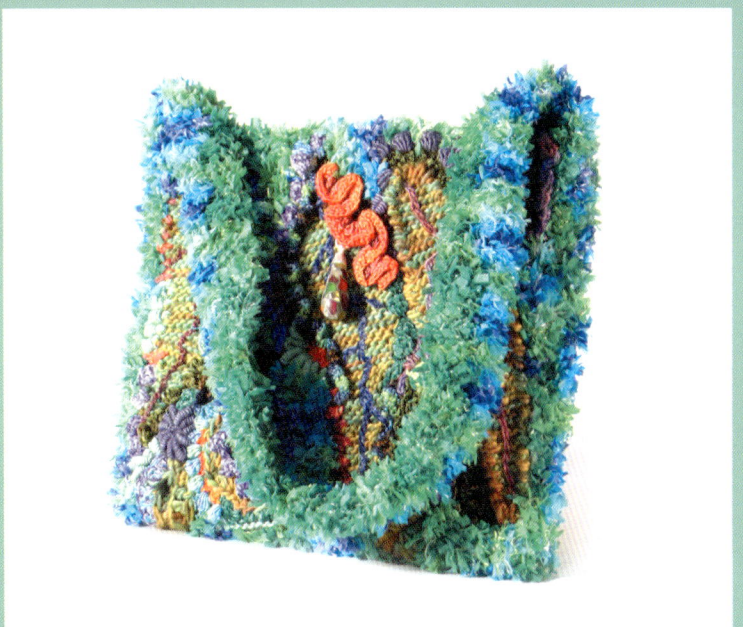

Crocheting into a length of mesh makes a firm shoulder strap

An extra leaf motif used as a flap closure

Abbreviations

ch   chain

dc   double crochet - in UK/Australian terminology, dc is equivalent to a US sc; in US terminology, dc is equivalent to a UK tr.

dtr   double treble - in UK/Australian terminology, dtr is equivalent to a US tr

htr   half treble (UK term - this is the same as a US hdc)

hdc   half double crochet (US term - this is the same as the UK htr)

st   stitch

sl st   slip stitch

tr   treble - in UK/Australian terminolory, tr is equivalent to a US dc; in US terminology, tr (triple) is equivalent to a UK dtr

For more information on Prudence's work, visit her website:
www.knotjustknitting.com

To learn more about Freeform methods for crochet and knitting, read:

Freeform: Serendipitous Design Techniques for Knitting and Crochet
by Prudence Mapstone
ISBN 0-9580443-0-9

To learn more about the crochet bullion stitch, read:

Bullions & Beyond: tips & techniques for the crochet bullion stitch
by Prudence Mapstone
ISBN 0-9580443-1-7

Join In
When you have made your own original handbag, why not join the
'A Girl can Never have Too Many Handbags' discussion group at:
http://groups.yahoo.com/group/AGirlCanNeverHaveTooManyHandbags

and exhibit your bag in one of the online exhibitions at:
http://handbags.knotjustknitting.com

the shaped bag frames used for many of the bags
in this book are available from:

Threads & More

141 Boundary Road
Bardon   Qld   4065   Australia
07 3367 0864
http://www.threadsandmore.com.au

Lacis

3163 Adeline Street
Berkeley   CA   94703   USA
510-843-7178
http://www.lacis.com